Bill Clinton

AND HIS PRESIDENCY

Bill Clinton
AND HIS PRESIDENCY

ELAINE LANDAU

A FIRST BOOK

Franklin Watts
A Division of Grolier Publishing
New York London Hong Kong Sydney
Danbury, Connecticut

Photographs ©: Clinton /Gore '96 General Committee, Inc.: 46; Corbis-Bettmann: 22, 50; Gamma-Liaison: 37 (Gehring), cover, 3, 49 (Diana Walker); International Media Exchange/Corbis-Bettmann: 12; Reuters/Corbis-Bettmann: 8, 13, 16, 20, 21, 25, 28, 30, 32, 33, 34, 39, 41, 42, 43, 45, 51, 52; UPI/Corbis-Bettmann: 17.

Landau, Elaine.
    Bill Clinton and his presidency / by Elaine Landau.
    p. cm.—(A First book)
    Includes bibliographical references index.
    Summary: Examines Bill Clinton's first four years in office as president, including his work on domestic affairs and foreign relations.
    ISBN 0-531-20295-X (lib.bdg.)   0-531-15841-1 (pbk.)
    1. Clinton, Bill, 1946—Juvenile literature. 2. United States—Politics and government—1993—Juvenile literature. 3. Clinton, Bill, 1946—Computer network resources—Juvenile literature. [1. Clinton, Bill, 1946–.
2. Presidents.
3. United States—Politics and government—1993–] 1. Title. II. Series
E885.L36 1997   96-37870
973.929'092—dc21   CIP
                                                        AC

Contents

★

Chapter 1

November 5, 1996 was both an exciting and a historic day in America. President Bill Clinton had just been reelected to the presidency. For the first time since 1936, a Democratic president had won a second term in office. It was also the first time in the nation's history that a Democrat was elected president while the Republicans controlled Congress.

Bill Clinton had achieved his goal, but it had been a long, uphill struggle from the president's modest beginnings. His father, William Jefferson Blythe III, an automobile salesman, had married his mother Virginia Cassidy Blythe in the early 1940s. Clinton's mother later described their first meeting as love at first sight, but their union was not destined to last. While she was pregnant with their first child, William Blythe was killed in an automobile accident.

Three months later on August 19, 1946, Virginia Cassidy Blythe gave birth to a baby boy she named William Jefferson after his father. As a widow and single parent, Clinton's mother worried about providing for her son. Although she was already a nurse, she knew that with more advanced

**Young Bill Clinton near his
childhood home of Hope, Arkansas**

training she would be able to earn considerably more money. Leaving her young son in his grandparents' care, Clinton's mother traveled to New Orleans to train as a nurse-*anesthetist*.[1]

Although Bill Clinton lived with his grandparents in the small town of Hope, Arkansas, for only the first few years of his life, the elderly couple played a valuable role in his upbringing. The boy's grandparents began his religious training and encouraged his natural sense of curiosity and love of learning. But while Clinton's grandparents were hopeful about his future, they never imagined that one day he would campaign as "the man from Hope" and eventually lead the nation.

Chapter 2

As a small child, Bill Clinton learned that accepting change is sometimes the key to surviving and thriving. This lesson would be crucial to him as president, but it also served him well during his youth. By the time Clinton turned four years old, his life had already changed dramatically. After becoming a nurse-anesthetist, his mother remarried. Her new husband, Roger Clinton, was a car dealer. Following their wedding, young Bill Clinton moved with his mother and stepfather to Hot Springs, Arkansas.

Once in school, Clinton proved to be an outstanding student earning As in even the more difficult subjects. As he grew older, he developed an interest in music. Bill Clinton took up the saxophone and won first prize in a statewide music competition. Those close to him saw that young Clinton never shunned a challenge—he learned to play every type of music from the classics to jazz.

At just nine years of age, Bill Clinton showed a keen interest in politics. He paid close attention to the televised presidential national conventions and followed political stories in the newspapers. In the summer of 1963, when Clinton was almost seventeen years old, he participated in Boys State, a program in which selected high school students study the political process. He won the honor of becoming a delegate to Boys Nation, and along with youths from around the country, he visited Washington, D.C., to see democracy in action. While at the nation's capital in July 1963, Bill Clinton had an opportunity to meet and shake hands with President John F. Kennedy, whom he had long admired. Seventeen-year-old Clinton returned home from that trip with a firm sense of purpose. His future, he believed, would be in government.

But though Clinton had already made his career choice, his life didn't always go smoothly. As a teenager he felt responsible for his mother and half brother Roger, who was born when Clinton was ten years old. Clinton even legally changed his name from Blythe to Clinton so the younger boy would feel more comfortable at school. But that proved to be the least of the family's problems.

Roger Clinton Sr. was an alcoholic who sometimes lashed out at young Clinton's mother and half brother. Unable to tolerate their being abused, Bill Clinton confronted his stepfather during one of his drunken outbursts. Standing in front of his mother and half brother, Clinton told his stepfather, "If you want them you'll have to go through me."[1] Roger Clinton Sr.'s violence stopped, but he continued drinking. Although Bill Clinton's mother often left her husband, she always forgave him and returned.

While in high school, Clinton left his personal problems outside the classroom. He became a member of the National Honor Society and a National Merit Scholarship semifi-

**In 1963, Clinton met President
John F. Kennedy and shook his hand.**

As a teenager, Bill Clinton (left) felt responsible for his mother and half brother.

nalist. After graduating from high school among the top ten students in his class, Clinton attended Georgetown University in Washington, D.C. To pay for college tuition and room and board, he had to work part-time. But Clinton graduated, winning a highly sought after honor—a Rhodes Scholarship.

The scholarship permitted Clinton to study at Oxford University in England from 1968 to 1970. For the first time in his life, he could pursue his education without needing a job to help cover costs. During this enriching and exciting time, Clinton took a variety of courses, traveled extensively, and read hundreds of books.

Yet two incidents occurred during this time that cast a shadow over his political career. The first involved Clinton's opposition to the war in Vietnam. He loved his country but firmly believed U.S. involvement in Vietnam was morally wrong. While in England, Clinton worked with other young men and women to organize opposition to the war.

During his first year at Oxford, however, Clinton received a letter from his draft board telling him to report for duty. Since the date he was to report had already passed by the time he received the letter, Clinton wrote back to ask for further instructions. In response, the draft board granted Clinton a student *draft deferment* for the rest of the school year.

When Bill Clinton returned to Arkansas that summer, he considered not going back to England for a second year. Instead, he thought he might go to the University of Arkansas Law School and enroll in the Reserve Officers' Training Corps (ROTC) on campus. This would allow him to receive his military training while attending law school.

Years later, Clinton's political opponents and critics would accuse him of enrolling in ROTC to avoid fighting in Vietnam. They argued that Clinton only joined ROTC because he suspected that by the time he finished law school and his ROTC training, the war would be over. Ironically, Clinton ultimately returned to England for the second year and canceled his ROTC enrollment. This made him eligible for active duty, but by then draftees were being selected by a lottery system. As Clinton set sail for England he didn't know whether or not his lottery number would be picked, but as it turned out, his number was never drawn.[2]

The second issue that Clinton's opponents would dwell on in later years had to do with drugs. While in England, Clinton tried marijuana once or twice. He later insisted that it hadn't been a pleasant experience and that he hadn't even inhaled. But his opponents still stressed that he had experimented with illegal drugs and was therefore an unfit role model for America's youth.

Following his return from England, Clinton attended Yale Law School in New Haven, Connecticut. There he met Hillary Rodham, a fellow student whom he would later marry. After graduating from law school, Clinton returned to Arkansas where he launched his political career. He proved to be an able campaigner—his outstanding public speaking skills helped him win broad support, and in him voters claimed to feel a genuine warmth and concern for people.

Bill Clinton was elected to the office of *attorney general* of Arkansas in 1976, and two years later, at just thirty-two years of age, he became governor of Arkansas. This victory made Clinton the youngest governor in the United States. Although he lost his bid for reelection in 1980 to his Republican opponent, he won the office back in 1982 with 55 percent of the vote.

These years were busy and productive for Bill Clinton. He dramatically improved education throughout Arkansas and instituted other important reforms. Clinton's family grew as well. In 1980, he and his wife Hillary were blessed with the birth of a daughter, Chelsea Victoria.

Yet in reality, Bill Clinton did not lead as charmed a life

Throughout his political career, Clinton's ability to reach voters on a personal level has contributed to his success. Here, he listens to the concerns of welfare mothers.

**Bill Clinton as governor of Arkansas early in 1979.
At age thirty-two, he was the youngest
governor in the United States.**

as many supposed. During his second term as governor, his half brother Roger Clinton Jr. served more than a year in prison for his involvement in an illegal drug operation. In addition, rumors circulated that the Clintons were having marital difficulties and that Bill Clinton had been seeing other women.

Following his half brother's prison release, the entire family sought counseling. For the first time, Clinton began to deal with some of the painful feelings he had pushed aside during his years of "success." Sadly, living with his alcoholic stepfather had taken a great personal toll on him. Clinton confided that at the age of sixteen he felt that he had to take on the responsibilities of a forty year old.

Chapter 3

Despite his personal problems, Clinton's zest for the American political scene never waned. He considered trying for the Democratic nomination for president in 1988, but decided against it. His daughter, Chelsea, was only seven years old at the time, and Clinton didn't want to spend a lot of time away from her on the campaign trail.

By the time Clinton won his fifth term as governor in 1990, he was a well-known political figure. His youth and vigor inspired many to look upon him as a new breed of Democrat. In July 1992 at the Democratic National Convention, he received his party's nomination for president. That November, he would try to defeat the Republican *incumbent* President George Bush and independent candidate H. Ross Perot.

The young candidate from Arkansas faced many challenges early in the campaign. His opponents labeled Clinton a draft dodger and brought up his experimentation with marijuana. They publicized charges made by some young women that Clinton had cheated on his wife with them. In

Bill Clinton, his wife, Hillary (left), and their daughter, Chelsea, watch the Democratic National Convention as the party nominates him to be their presidential candidate in 1992.

While running for president, Clinton had to answer many tough questions posed by his critics and the media.

response, Bill and Hillary Clinton appeared together on national TV to clear up matters. They stated that although they had endured some marital difficulties, they remained committed to making their relationship a success. As Bill Clinton put it, "We never wanted to give up on each other and we still don't."[1]

**Bound for his inauguration in Washington, D.C.,
president-elect Clinton and family wave good-bye
to a crowd gathered at Little Rock Airport in Arkansas.**

Meanwhile Clinton and his vice presidential choice, Tennessee Senator Albert Gore Jr., campaigned throughout the country. Clinton's plans for the United States included reforming the health care and welfare systems, reducing energy use, and introducing tax cuts for most Americans. Some voters, including women, minority group members, and workers who felt excluded or ignored by President Bush and the Republican party, were drawn to Clinton's dream for America. And on November 3, 1992, he was elected to the office of president.

Clinton saw his victory as the dawn of a new day in America. Victory parties erupted throughout the president's home state of Arkansas as well as at Clinton campaign headquarters across the nation. Clinton supporters danced in the aisles to the song that had become Clinton's theme—"Don't Stop Thinking About Tomorrow." For many, the Clinton win represented more than just the victory of a deserving candidate; it heralded a younger, more idealistic generation coming to power. On the eve of his victory, no one wanted to think about the obstacles ahead for the forty-second president of the United States.

Chapter 4

ANYTHING IS POSSIBLE

The excitement that electrified election night carried over into Clinton's descent on Washington, D.C. He believed he had received a *mandate* from the people to enact broad, sweeping changes. During a State of the Union address early in his term of office, Clinton told the American people, "Tonight I want to talk to you about what government can do because I believe government must do more."[1]

The nation's new first lady, Hillary Rodham Clinton, shared her husband's vision for the country. Many Clinton supporters saw Mrs. Clinton as a breath of fresh air in Washington, D.C. The traditional role of the first lady as a quiet, comforting background presence did not seem to fit Hillary Clinton, who had been described as a "dynamic young lawyer with big ideas about social change and an overt governing partnership with her husband."[2]

Hillary Rodham Clinton hoped to shatter stereotypes about where "a woman's place" was. She reportedly told friends that she "wanted above all to do good . . . be a role model for all women and . . . prove that gender need not be a crippling limitation."[3]

The Clintons flip the switch to light the national Christmas
tree during their first Christmas at the White House.

Despite the new president's optimism and energy, his administration quickly suffered some serious setbacks. In fact, some political scientists believe that the "anything is possible" phase of President Clinton's first term in office lasted only from his *inauguration* until November 1994. The new president, who had described himself as an agent of change, saw many of his tireless efforts fail to produce the desired effects. To Clinton's disappointment, this period of his presidency has largely been viewed as one of disastrous appointments and minor scandals.

Clinton's first choice for attorney general quickly drew fire. In the story that later became known as Nannygate, it was revealed that the woman Clinton sought to appoint to the nation's top law enforcement position had actually broken the law herself. Zoe Baird, the appointee, openly admitted to both administration officials and the senators who interviewed her that she had employed *undocumented workers* as a nanny and chauffeur. Baird and some officials in the administration merely viewed her action as a minor judgment error. But when all the facts came to light, the American public was enraged.

Allegedly, Baird and her husband had a net worth of more than two million dollars. Besides having hired illegal workers, the couple had also failed to pay the Social Security and worker's compensation taxes they owed the government. Rather than being viewed as a working mother desperately in need of quality child care, Zoe Baird suddenly came to symbolize the rich, privileged class of Americans who either ignore or rewrite existing laws and rules to suit themselves.

President Clinton found himself in an embarrassing position. Only a month before at his inauguration he had vowed "to reform our politics so that power and privilege no longer shut down the voice of the people."[4] Now the calls and letters coming into the White House regarding Baird's confirmation opposed it overwhelmingly. One California parent summed up public sentiment: "We have people who can't put food on their tables who commit crimes and get hammered. Then you have a person who doesn't have to worry about that and makes an unethical choice and we want to make them attorney general. I can't put the two of those together very well."[5]

Within a week of her nomination, Baird became the first U.S. cabinet nominee ever to withdraw from consideration for a post. The fiasco left the new president looking worse for the experience.

After some other possible nominees were considered and rejected, Janet Reno was appointed to the position. While there was nothing unsettling in her background, Ms. Reno did not escape controversy for long. In the spring of 1993, the FBI conducted a raid on the Branch Davidian compound (a religious group's commune) in Waco, Texas. The FBI attack, which resulted in considerable casualties among the Branch Davidians, was later deemed overly assaultive. Janet Reno, who had been on the job for only a month, took full responsibility for the action, claiming that any errors were her fault.

Although President Clinton had been fully briefed on the matter, he was careful to distance himself from the catastrophe. When questioned by reporters on the morning of the assault about whether he knew of the FBI plan, Clinton replied, "I was aware of it. I think the attorney general made the decision." After being pressed further he said only, "I

Clinton and Vice President Al Gore accompany attorney general nominee Janet Reno to a press conference.

knew it was going to be done, but the decisions were entirely theirs."[6] Clinton's critics felt the president should have shared the blame with Reno.

The early days of the Clinton administration were also darkened by a number of somewhat scandalous incidents that caught the media's attention. These include what came to be known as the President's $5,500 haircut. The actual cost of the haircut by the fashionable stylist Christophe of Beverly Hills was $200.00. But the styling took place aboard Air Force One (the presidential jet), which idled at Los Angeles Airport for about an hour with a full crew aboard at a cost of $5,300.

The day before, in New Mexico, Clinton had gotten his sideburns and neck shaved and had some makeup applied for a personal appearance. When a White House official heard about these extravagances he exclaimed, "He got his neck shaved? He might as well as got it cut."[7] Presidential scholar Stephen Hess echoed these sentiments: "The President should remind himself that the people who elected him get their hair cut not styled, by barbers named Ed not Christophe, and they pay in cash not personal services contracts."[8]

But the President's haircut seemed minor compared to other questionable matters connected to the Clintons. In the case that became known as Travelgate, the Clintons fired White House travel office staff members who they believed were guilty of improper conduct. An *audit* by an independent accounting firm, which revealed numerous fiscal abuses within the travel department, justified the dismissals, but the Clintons ended up looking bad anyway.

The Clintons failed to take into account that the dismissed staffers had a powerful ally—the White House press corps. Travel office staffers had seen to it that members of the White House press corps flew first class and were served their favorite drinks as soon as they were seated. Items purchased during these trips were flown back free of charge, and press corps family members could come along for only a nominal charge.

Although Clinton's first two years in office were plagued by several failed appointments, other appointments during this period have proved very successful, such as the naming of Ruth Bader Ginsburg to the Supreme Court.

The press attack on the Clintons for indirectly threatening the "extras" they and others had long enjoyed seemed relentless. The press cast Mrs. Clinton as the sinister force behind the move and accused her and the president of planning to fill the newly vacant positions with their supporters from Little Rock, Arkansas.

The unflattering publicity continued in July 1993 with the suicide of White House deputy counsel Vince Foster. Foster, who had come to Washington with the Clintons, had been a longtime friend of the president and first lady. Reportedly, Foster had been extremely concerned that the White House's handling of the travel office dismissals would lead to Congressional hearings on the matter. At the time of his suicide, Foster was reportedly overworked and downtrodden. He had told friends and associates that he needed additional support staff and that he was afraid of letting "the President and Hillary down."[9]

Vince Foster's death raised a number of disturbing issues about the Clintons. But the most troublesome was Foster's role in a questionable Arkansas land deal, known as Whitewater, that the Clintons had been involved in. Whitewater proved to be a thorny issue for Bill and Hillary Clinton into the president's second term as others involved were convicted of fraud and other offenses.

However, the most destructive blow to the Clinton's early dream of building a better nation came with the crushing defeat of their plan for health care reform. Mrs. Clinton had worked for months to devise the massive health care proposal that would involve an overhaul of the country's medical resources. However, the first lady had largely worked alone on the reform package without securing the aid of potential supporters. She and the president had also failed to build a firm consensus on the changes before attempting to push the bill through Congress. The result was disastrous. The monumental reform that was to alter health care in America and serve as an everlasting tribute to the Clinton administration died in Congressional committees.

The president and first lady's health care reform package brought frustration and failure to the administration, prompting Clinton to rethink his approach to policy-making.

Despite some setbacks, Clinton did succeed in passing important bills during the early years of his first term, including the Brady Bill, which requires a five-day waiting period before the purchase of a handgun. Here, President Clinton signs the Brady Bill into law as James Brady, the bill's namesake, looks on.

To many, Mrs. Clinton had become a member of the "big government ruling class." As historian Michael Bischloss described her fate, "The more the first lady is in the public eye, the more she is into substantive power, the more uneasy the public becomes."[10]

In response to the heavy Democratic losses in the 1994 congressional elections, Clinton promised to reform White House policy to better reflect the needs and desires of voters.

The first two years of his term had hardly been what Bill Clinton had in mind for America when he took office. And in the 1994 Congressional elections, he paid for what voters perceived as fumbling, errors, and an attempted "big government" takeover. Across the country, Americans swept sizable numbers of Democrats out of the House and Senate, replacing them with young Republican congresspeople.

The people's message to the Clintons was undeniable; they used the ballot box to reject the president's approach to leading the country. But Bill Clinton was not about to give up. After accepting the blame for the Democrat's loss in Congress, he set about remaking himself into what the American people wanted.

Chapter 5

THE COMEBACK

As a young politician Bill Clinton had more than once been called "the Comeback Kid." Just as it had in the past, his ability to react to change and adapt proved invaluable following the 1994 Congressional elections. Vestiges of big government, such as the first lady's massive health care package, disappeared from the administration's agenda. "You can do too many things at the same time," the president told reporters as he reflected on the last two years. "Sometimes when you're trying to do something really big like health care, you have to do it piece by piece."[1]

One such small piece of health care reform was the Kennedy-Kassenbaum bill, which President Clinton enthusiastically signed. This legislation allows workers to take their health insurance with them when they change jobs. It was the type of piecemeal step the Clintons would have previously rejected in favor of more sweeping change, but the bill fit perfectly with the administration's new philosophy.

The president's greatest successes usually resulted from small, well-planned steps. Among Clinton's foremost

Clinton made up for the rocky beginning
to his term by coming out strong in 1995.

achievements was cutting the nation's *deficit* while maintaining a healthy economy. The deficit decline—an impressive 60 percent from two hundred and ninety billion dollars in 1992 to about one hundred and sixteen billion in 1996—was even greater than Clinton expected.

The unemployment rate also declined during the president's first term, from 7 percent when Clinton took office to about 5.4 percent at the start of his second term. While President Clinton's campaign pledge had been to create eight million new jobs for Americans, closer to ten million new positions now existed. Also to Clinton's credit, the inflation rate stayed under three percent throughout his first term of office. This four-year stretch was the longest period in thirty years in which the inflation rate had remained both low and constant. Presidential aide George Stephanopoulus praised Clinton's handling of the economy with this comment: "We wouldn't be where we are today without the tough decisions he made."[2]

The President also scored points with voters when he stood firm against what some saw as an overreaching Republican Congress trying to enact a harsh legislative program in record time. Much of the public worried that the Republicans might cut Medicare and other popular programs. Although the polls indicated that most people did not fully support the Republican "revolution" (as the proposed legislation was called), Speaker of the House Newt Gingrich failed to acknowledge the waning support for his agenda.

Feeling certain that the public was behind him, President Clinton vetoed tough Congressional spending bills he felt would be too hard on most Americans. Before long, the

Clinton's popularity soared when he stood firm against what many saw as overly harsh budget cuts by the Republican congress led by Senate Majority Leader Bob Dole (left) and Speaker of the House Newt Gingrich (right).

Republican Congress and the President were trapped in a budget deadlock, causing the government to shut down. Even on the day before the impending government shutdown, Clinton held his ground. As the midnight deadline neared, the President stated, "I will not now, not ever, sign this budget. I think it's bad for America."[3]

The view of the Republicans as extremists and Clinton as the last defender of the elderly became the centerpiece of the Democratic party's TV and newspaper ads at the time. Overall, the public sided with the president, believing that the Republicans were responsible for shutting down the government and that they intended to finance tax cuts for the rich by severely reducing health care for the elderly.

Clinton never wavered in his stand, and two months after an acceptable compromise was reached the press declared the President the winner in the budget battle. His popularity rating soared by 50 percent and remained high. The 1995 budget fight had actually served as Bill Clinton's first bid for reelection. But the President and his advisors knew they had to implement further image and policy changes to ensure a second term in office.

In April 1995, following the terrorist bombing in Oklahoma City, Clinton used the presidency to unite Americans in a time of crisis. During his visit to the site, he mourned for those killed, promised to catch those responsible, and reassured a devastated city and a shocked nation. He appeared both presidential and sympathetic—just what the country needed to begin to heal itself.

The press and the public witnessed "a new Bill Clinton" emerging from the turmoil of the first half of his term. His critics charged that the changes were merely strategic reelection ploys. But those close to him claimed to see a genuine *metamorphosis* in the president. National leadership had matured Clinton, and he now saw the world and his role as president of the United States differently. Many who knew him felt the president had personally grown a great deal. Since being elected to office, he'd had to con-

While in office, Clinton suffered the loss of several people close to him, including his friend and commerce secretary Ron Brown, who died in a plane crash while promoting U.S. business interests overseas. Many speculate that these tragedies have had a maturing influence on Clinton.

tend with the death of his mother, the death of his friend and commerce secretary Ron Brown, the suicide of his good friend Vince Foster, and the assassination of Israel's prime minister Yitzhak Rabin, to whom he had become extremely close.

As president, Clinton also had assumed an important role in the world arena. While working for peace in the Mid-

Clinton presided over many peace negotiations, including several in the Middle East. At the signing of a historic peace agreement between the Israelis and Palestinians in 1993, Yitzhak Rabin (left), prime minister of Israel, shakes hands with PLO Chairman Yasser Arafat (right) as Clinton looks on.

dle East, he negotiated the Israel-Jordan Peace Treaty and helped the Israelis and Palestinians hammer out a historic peace agreement. Also, the President and twenty-nine world and regional leaders organized a March 1996 Summit of Peacemakers in Egypt to support the Middle East peace process and counteract terrorism.

Clinton applauds as King Hussein of Jordan (left) shakes hands with Yitzhak Rabin of Israel (right) in 1994, symbolizing peace between the two nations. Rabin, a noble peacemaker and close friend of Bill Clinton, was assassinated in Israel the following year.

To boost America's economy, President Clinton fought for strong trade agreements throughout the world. This led to increased opportunities for U.S. exporters. Exports grew 31 percent during his first term.

As commander in chief of the United States Armed Forces, Clinton shouldered the responsibility of sending

25,000 troops to Bosnia's war zone. The lives and welfare of U.S. soldiers sent to Africa, the Middle East, and other parts of the world also weighed heavily on his mind. Yet when necessary, Clinton made the tough calls and lived with the consequences. "I have a much better ability now to deal with the ups and down and pressures of the presidency," Clinton told reporters at the close of his first term in office.[4]

Undeniably, the "new" Bill Clinton is a more moderate president than the man elected in 1992. His move toward the political center is evident in the legislation passed during his first term. Clinton pushed through an anti-crime bill in August 1994 to put more police officers on our nation's streets. This act will provide 100,000 additional federally funded police officers by the year 2000. To afford this measure, however, Clinton had to cut the number of federal employees and reduce the time inmates spend on death row before their execution.

Clinton further pleased moderates by fulfilling his campaign promise to reform welfare. He signed a welfare reform bill that limits how long a person can stay on welfare and attempts to force welfare recipients to work. Liberals viewed the measure as a risky experiment in social policy that may result in countless starving or malnourished American children. However, Clinton quelled the rage of disappointed voters by promising to soften the harshest parts of the legislation. In the future, he has said he intends to stop the reduction of food stamps and make legal immigrants eligible for benefits.

By the second half of her husband's first term, the first lady had changed as well. While insiders still feel she's an important force in the White House, Hillary Rodham Clinton

44

Several times in his first term, Clinton had to use his authority as commander in chief of the U.S. military. Here, a stern President Clinton is photographed moments after he announced to the nation that U.S. missiles had been launched at Iraqi military intelligence targets.

Both the president and first lady have changed during Clinton's first term.

now keeps a lower profile. She has always been an ardent advocate for children, but her more recent handiwork is usually less obvious.

Mrs. Clinton has also traveled to various parts of the globe developing an international network of professional women. Many abroad see her as "the first lady of the world," serving as a valued voice for women living in countries where they can't speak out for themselves.

Chapter 6

By November 1996, Bill Clinton was well positioned for reelection. Besides having always been an outstanding campaigner, his bid for a second term in office came at a time of peace and national prosperity.

Clinton and his campaign staff used all they had learned from his first term in office to shape the reelection campaign. As the President stressed his goals of balancing the budget and further cutting the deficit, many characterized him as a Democrat running on a moderate Republican agenda. His support of school uniforms and requiring 16 year olds applying for driver's licenses to take drug tests bolstered his moderate image.

At seventy three, the Republican presidential candidate, former Senator Robert Dole, was considerably older than Clinton. And although President Ronald Reagan was about Dole's age when he ran for president, Reagan always gave the impression of looking to the future while Dole seemed to be trying to recapture the best of the past. But regardless of a candidate's age and attitude, running against

A confident President Clinton campaigns in Rhode Island for a second term in office.

a popular incumbent in good economic times is always difficult.

Nevertheless, the media offered many reasons for Dole's defeat. Some said that Dole had spent so much money and energy trying to win the Republican nomination that not enough remained for the actual election. Popular opinion also held that Clinton had a superior campaign staff and that Dole had stressed the wrong issues. Liberal Republicans argued that Gingrich and his unpopular extremist

President Clinton debates his Republican opponent, Bob Dole. Clinton maintained a sizable lead throughout the campaign.

policies had hindered Dole's chances. They felt that by voting for Clinton, the public actually was rejecting Gingrich.

Clinton's reelection team had been extremely well prepared. They countered attacks on the President's morality by encouraging voters to view family values on a broader level. TV and newspaper ads stressed that Clinton's fervor

Some people thought that Clinton's victory was in part a rejection of Speaker of the House Newt Gingrich, pictured here with President Clinton in 1995.

The Clintons still have obstacles to face, but as in the past, they will likely persevere.

for enhanced maternity benefits and extended parental leave affirmed his support for family values. Their underlying message was, "We're pro-family because we want to use the federal government to help your family."[1] Charges of the

President's past infidelity no longer seemed as relevant to many voters.

Although Clinton won the election, his path to an enviable place in history is not guaranteed. An independent counsel has been appointed by the Justice Department to investigate the Clintons' part in Whitewater and Mrs. Clinton's role in the travel office firings.[2] Unanswered questions also remain about the hiring of a former bar bouncer named Craig Livingstone as White House security chief. Accusations that he improperly obtained FBI files for White House use still haunt the administration. In addition, a controversy surfaced during Clinton's reelection campaign over foreign contributions to the Democratic party and possible campaign finance law violations.

The Clintons, however, have risen above rumors and scandals in the past and hope to do so in the future. It's likely that Clinton's second term will center on specifically geared legislation; the president's immediate plans include some well-placed tax cuts, providing health insurance for all American children, and amending the harshest portions of the welfare reform bill.

As Clinton told the nation on the night of his reelection, "It is time to put politics aside, join together, and get the job done for America's future. Tonight we proclaim that the vital American center is alive and well. It is the common ground on which we have made our progress. . . . Now we've got a bridge to build and I'm ready if you are."[3]

Source Notes

CHAPTER 1

1. Don Baer, "Man-Child in Politics Land," *U.S. News & World Report* (October 14, 1991): 40.

CHAPTER 2

1. Bill Turque, "I Think We're Ready," *Newsweek* (February 3, 1992): 21.
2. Charles F. Allen and Jonathan Portis, *The Life and Career of Bill Clinton: The Comeback Kid* (New York: Birch Lane Press, 1992), 29.

CHAPTER 3

1. Eleanor Clift, "Political Ambitions, Personal Choices," *Newsweek* (March 9, 1992): 36.

CHAPTER 4

1. George J. Church, "The Learning Curve," *Time* (September 2, 1996): 32.
2. Kenneth T. Walsh, "Her Time of Travail," *U.S. News & World Report* (February 5, 1996): 28.
3. Ibid.

4. Nancy Gibbs, "Thumbs Down," *Time* (February 1, 1993): 28.
5. Ibid.
6. Michael Kramer, "The First Hundred Days" *Time* (May 3, 1993): 46.
7. Margaret Carlsen, "Shear Dismay," *Time* (May 31, 1993): 21.
8. Ibid.
9. "The Last Days of Vince Foster," *Time* (March 18, 1996): 67.
10. Kenneth T. Walsh, "Her Time of Travail," *U.S. News & World Report* (February 5, 1996): 28.

CHAPTER 5

1. Kenneth T. Walsh, "Coming of Age," *U.S. News & World Report* (September 2, 1996): 24.
2. George J. Church, "The Learning Curve," *Time* (September 2, 1996): 33.
3. Howard Fineman, "On Target," *Newsweek* (November 18, 1996): 54.
4. Howard Fineman and Bill Turque, "How He Got His Groove," *Newsweek* (September 2, 1996): 20.

CHAPTER 6

1. David Wagner, "Clinton Policy Plans Await Second Term," *Insight* (November 25, 1996): 13.
2. R. Emmett Tyrrell, Jr., *Boy Clinton: The Political Biography* (Washington, D.C.: Regnery Publishing, Inc., 1996), 240.
3. Howard Fineman, "Hail and Farewell," *Newsweek* (November 18, 1996): 8.

Glossary

anesthetist - a person trained to give anesthetics or drugs that deaden pain.

attorney general - the head law enforcement official of a nation or state.

audit - an examination of financial accounts to determine their correctness.

deficit - the amount of money lacking from a specific or predetermined sum.

draft deferment - a status that prevents an individual from being drafted into the armed services for a specific period of time.

inauguration - a formal ceremony during which a person is inducted into office.

incumbent - a person seeking reelection to an office he already holds.

mandate - an order from the public to an elected official or legislative body to take a specific course of action.

metamorphosis - changing from one thing into another.

undocumented workers - workers who are not citizens of the United States and who have not obtained the documents required for working legally in the United States.

Further Reading

★

Blue, Rose and Corinne J. Naden. *The White House Kids*. Brookfield, CT: The Millbrook Press, 1995.

Cole, Michael D. *John F. Kennedy: President of the New Frontier*. Springfield, NJ: Enslow Publishers, 1996.

Faber, Doris. *Eleanor Roosevelt: First Lady of the World*. New York: Viking, 1985.

Greene, Carol. *Bill Clinton: Forty-Second President of the United States*. Danbury, CT: Children's Press, 1995.

Hewett, Joan. *Getting Elected: The Diary of a Campaign*. New York: Lodestar, 1989.

Kent, Zachary. *William Jefferson Clinton: Forty-Second President of the United States*. Danbury, CT: Children's Press, 1994.

LeVert, Suzanne. *Hillary Rodham Clinton*. Brookfield, CT: The Millbrook Press, 1994.

Mayo, Edith P., ed. *The Smithsonian Book of First Ladies: Their Lives, Times and Issues*. New York: Henry Holt, 1994.

Smith, Carter, ed. *Presidents in a Time of Change: A Sourcebook on the U.S. Presidency*. Brookfield, CT: The Millbrook Press, 1993.

Smith, Carter, ed. *The Founding Presidents: A Sourcebook on the U.S. Presidency*. Brookfield, CT: The Millbrook Press, 1993.

Internet Resources

Because of the changeable nature of the Internet, sites appear and disappear very quickly. These resources offered useful information on Bill Clinton and the U.S. Government at the time of publication. Internet addresses must be entered with capital and lowercase letters exactly as they appear.

YAHOO!
http://www.yahoo.com/
The *Yahoo!* directory of the World Wide Web is an excellent place to find Internet sites on any topic.

THE WHITE HOUSE HOME PAGE
http://www.whitehouse.gov/
This site highlights the lives and accomplishments of the president and vice president, features an online tour of the White House, and offers information about all facets of the executive branch of government.

THE SENATE HOME PAGE
http://www.senate.gov/

THE HOUSE OF REPRESENTATIVES HOME PAGE
http://www.house.gov/

These sites offers information about the history of the U.S. Senate and the House of Representatives and detail recent legislation considered in Congress. Both sites feature links to your local congresspeople, allowing you to examine their voting records and send them e-mail.

CONTACTING THE PRESIDENT OVER THE INTERNET

You can send e-mail to the President and First Lady through the White House home page, or you can e-mail them directly using these addresses:

President: **president@whitehouse.gov**

First Lady: **first.lady@whitehouse.gov**

Index

Italicized page numbers indicate illustrations.

About the Author

★

Popular author Elaine Landau worked as a newspaper reporter, an editor, and a youth services librarian before becoming a full-time writer. She has written more than ninety nonfiction books for young people, including *Alzheimer's Disease* and *Stalking*. Ms. Landau, who has a bachelor's degree in English and journalism from New York University and a master's degree in library and information science from Pratt Institute, lives in Florida with her husband and son.